SIDE BY SIDE

SIDE BY SIDE

Five Favorite Picture-Book Teams Go to Work

LEONARD S. MARCUS

Walker & Company

New York

For Lynn Saville and Philip Fried

ACKNOWLEDGMENTS

My first thanks go to the writers and artists about whom I have written in these pages.
I thank them for the candor, patience, professionalism, permissions granted,
and, not least, the spirit of collaboration they brought to the work.
I also wish to acknowledge with gratitude the help of the following
individuals and institutions: Kate Boyle and Peter Nelson of The Jones Library
(Amherst, Massachusetts), Phyllis Fogelman of Phyllis Fogelman Books,
Eric Lindbloom, Myles C. Pinkney, Tom Polapink of the Old Rhinebeck Aerodrome,
Milan Sabatini, Todd Weinstein, Nancy Willard, and Linda Zuckerman.

I thank my agent George M. Nicholson for his warm friendship and wise counsel.
I thank my friend and editor Emily Easton and the staff of Walker & Company
for their unwavering support of this project, for their help in making the book
better, and for their commitment to all their authors.

I thank my wife, Amy, and my son, Jacob, for their love.

First published in the United States of America in 2001 by
Walker Publishing Company, Inc.

Published simultaneously in Canada by Fitzhenry and Whiteside,
Markham, Ontario L3R 4T8

Jacket design and illustrations from *Louis the Fish* by Arthur Yorinks, jacket design and illustration by Richard Egielski. Cover art
and illustration copyright © 1980 by Richard Egielski. Reprinted by permission of Farrar, Straus and Giroux, LLC.

Jacket design and illustrations from *The Glorious Flight* by Alice and Martin Provensen, copyright © 1983 by Alice and Martin Provensen.
Used by permission of Viking Penguin, a division of Penguin Putnam Inc.

Jacket design and illustrations from *The Stinky Cheese Man and Other Fairly Stupid Tales* by Jon Scieszka, illustrated by Lane Smith,
copyright © 1992 by Lane Smith, illustrations. Used by permission of Viking Penguin, a division of Penguin Putnam Inc.

Jacket design and illustrations from *Sam and the Tigers* by Julius Lester, illustrated by Jerry Pinkney, copyright © 1996 Jerry Pinkney, art.
Used by permission of Dial Books for Young Readers, a division of Penguin Putnam Inc.

Jacket design and illustrations by Bruce Degen from *The Magic School Bus Explores the Senses* by Joanna Cole.
Illustration copyright © 1989 by Bruce Degen. Reprinted by permission of Scholastic Inc.
The Magic School Bus is a registered trademark of Scholastic Inc.

Photograph of Arthur Yorinks and Richard Egielski © Todd Weinstein; photograph of Martin and Alice Provensen © Eric Lindbloom;
photograph of Lane Smith and Jon Scieszka by Brian Smale, reproduced by permission of Penguin Putnam; photograph of Molly Leach,
courtesy of Molly Leach; photograph of Julius Lester © Milan Sabatini; photograph of Jerry Pinkney © Myles C. Pinkney;
photograph of Myles Pinkney © Jerry Pinkney; photograph of Joanna Cole and Bruce Degen, courtesy of Scholastic Inc.

Library of Congress Cataloging-in-Publication Data
Marcus, Leonard S., 1950–
Side by side : five favorite picture-book teams go to work / Leonard S. Marcus.
p. cm.
Includes bibliographical references and index.
Summary: Describes the process by which several teams of authors and illustrators have created such picture books
as "Louis the Fish," "The Glorious Flight," "The Stinky Cheese Man and Other Fairly Stupid Tales,"
"Sam and the Tigers," and "The Magic School Bus Explores the Senses."
ISBN 0-8027-8778-9 — ISBN 0-8027-8779-7 (lib. bdg.)
1. Picture books for children—Publishing—United States—Juvenile literature.
2. Authors, American—20th century—Juvenile literature. 3. Illustrators—United States—
Juvenile literature. 4. Children's literature—Authorship—Juvenile literature. 5. Children's literature—
Illustrations—Juvenile literature. [1. Picture books. 2. Authors, American. 3. Illustrators.] I. Title.
Z286.P53 M37 2001
070.5'73—dc21   2001026344

Book design by Claire Counihan

Printed in Hong Kong

2 4 6 8 10 9 7 5 3 1

CONTENTS

Introduction

Collaborators are people working together toward a common goal. All of us collaborate each time we take part in a team sport, sing in a choir, help bake a cake, or do a science project with a classmate. When writers and illustrators team up to make picture books, they become collaborators too. In the pages that follow, members of five long-running and extraordinary artist-writer collaborations talk about making picture books side by side.

Picture-book teams get started in a variety of ways. Some begin when friends—or friends of friends—decide to try their hand at working together. Notable picture books have been created by husband-and-wife teams: Ingri and Edgar Parin d'Aulaire, Clement and Edith Thacher Hurd, Leo and Diane Dillon, and Alice and Martin Provensen, to name a few.

Most picture-book teams come together in a more businesslike way: with a publisher accepting a writer's manuscript, then choosing an illustrator whose style seems a good match for it. Once the match has been made, the publishing company (including its editors, art directors, and others) works separately with the writer and the illustrator, guiding the book toward completion. As odd as it may seem, most artists and writers who are paired in this way *never* meet to discuss the book they are nonetheless creating together. Many publishers believe that keeping a distance between collaborators makes for smoother going. Collaborators may disagree with each other. They may not even like each other. Or they may simply feel freer to follow their own creative vision when working separately. For these reasons, the less personal arrangement favored by publishers often works well.

But there are always some writers and artists who prefer—or need—to be in the thick of a freewheeling give-and-take with their partners—at least some of the time. For them, collaboration is not only about contributing their ideas and skill with a paintbrush or pencil or computer. It is also about getting together and getting along.

Collaborators who work closely together must learn to trust and be patient with each other. They must know when to offer help, and when to let their partner solve things on his or her own. It may surprise you to learn how many different ways collaborators have of helping, or simply encouraging, each other. As often as not, literally working side by side matters less than feeling in harmony with a partner's ideas. Collaboration is an art in itself: Each team must invent its own way to pull together.

Not all friendships last. Neither do all collaborations. When a picture-book collaboration goes well, however, those involved come away with several rewards. Each collaborator can rightly take pride in having done his or her personal best. Each can feel glad about having contributed to a team effort. And each will have experienced the special thrill of having shared in the making of a book that readers may remember for years to come.

Arthur Yorinks

(born August 21, 1953, Roslyn, New York)

and

Richard Egielski

(born July 16, 1952, Queens, New York)

LOUIS THE FISH
(Farrar, Straus & Giroux, 1980)

Art medium:
watercolor

Arthur Yorinks (left)
and Richard Egielski

The story of how writer Arthur Yorinks met illustrator Richard Egielski is about as unlikely as anything that happens in the comically odd and dreamlike picture books they created together, starting in 1977 with *Sid and Sol*.

In 1974, as a senior at New York's Parsons School of Design, Egielski took a class in children's-book illustration with Maurice Sendak, famed creator of *Where the Wild Things Are*. By the time he completed the class and graduated later that year, Egielski knew that picture-book making was the life for him.

A year later, and still looking for his first job as a book illustrator, Egielski decided one day to visit his old teacher at Parsons.

"So, I'm in the elevator and suddenly this guy I don't know pokes me in the back and asks me if my name is Richard. I think, 'This is weird!' Then he says, 'I'm Arthur Yorinks and I write stories.' I think, 'Weirder and weirder!' Finally he says,

'Maurice Sendak has told me about you!' I still don't understand—but now I am really listening. Then Arthur explained how Maurice had told him that he hoped we would meet. He'd said he thought we might make good collaborators. There was just one problem. Maurice couldn't remember my last name! So he described me to Arthur instead, which he was able to do in incredible visual detail. And that's how when Arthur and I got into the elevator together at Parsons that afternoon, Arthur knew it was me."

Yorinks had copies of some of his stories with him that day and asked if Egielski would like to read them. "I said 'sure,' and went through the stories while he looked at my portfolio."

"When I saw Richard's drawings," Arthur Yorinks recalls, "I thought, 'Wow! A real artist!'"

Egielski remembers thinking: "'This is a nice guy and an interesting guy.' I liked Arthur's stories very much. One story I especially liked was called 'Sid and Sol.'"

A few years earlier, Yorinks had become friends with Maurice Sendak in an equally far-fetched way. After reading an article about Sendak in the *New York Times*, Yorinks, then sixteen, had decided to find some way to meet the celebrated artist. He was thunderstruck by what seemed like striking similarities between Sendak's childhood and his own. (Both had been youngest children growing up in Jewish households on the edge of New York. As youngsters, both had spent endless hours inventing stories while looking out the window and listening to music.) Yorinks was convinced that Sendak would understand his stories and would perhaps know what he should do with them.

When the scruffy-looking teen showed up uninvited one afternoon at the artist's door, Sendak politely turned him away but invited Arthur to telephone him. Unsure of how Sendak would react if he really did call, Yorinks hesitated— several times hanging up before finally, one evening, saying who was calling. That evening, he and Maurice Sendak had a long phone conversation. More conversations followed. They met for lunch. It was after reading Yorinks's stories that Sendak described for him his tall, rail-thin former art student. As Yorinks listened, he thought sadly that in a city as big as New York he would never find this "Richard" in a million years.

Once they did meet, however, it took Yorinks and Egielski little time to realize how alike they were in many ways. They admired the same picture-book artists (besides Sendak: Tomi Ungerer, Edward Gorey, and James Marshall); the same writers (novelists Franz Kafka and Nikolai Gogol). They liked the same television shows and movies (*Star Trek*, *King Kong*, and Alfred Hitchcock thrillers). They had grown up near each other in similar neighborhoods: Egielski in Queens, New York; Yorinks just over the border in Nassau County, Long Island. "We both saw Manhattan as the Emerald City—the Land of Oz," Egielski says. "It was an exciting time. We were two struggling young guys with tiny apartments, each trying to make it in New York City."

Exciting, but also frustrating—neither was having much luck finding a publisher.

"Editors didn't know what to make of my stories," Yorinks says.

"I painted with lots of browns and grays," says Egielski, "and I didn't have cute little characters in my portfolio. I had gone to Catholic parochial school, and I *did* have a drawing of a nun with a ruler chasing one of her students down the hall! So, I wasn't getting picture-book assignments from publishers, who thought my work was too dark."

Each was determined to succeed and had decided by then that their best chance of doing so lay in finding someone to team up with. Each had good reason to think so. At the age of ten or eleven, Yorinks and a friend had made a comic book together and loved the experience. Egielski recalls: "When I was fourteen, I discovered *The Hobbit*

and began drawing my own illustrations for Tolkien's fantasy. In a sense, that was my first experience of working with a collaborator. Drawing for me became a really cool way of getting deeper into the things I was reading."

Illustration by a teenaged Richard Egielski for chapter 8 of J. R. R. Tolkien's *The Hobbit*, in which Bombur is pulled to safety from the enchanted stream by his fellow dwarves.

They decided to do *Sid and Sol* on their own and worry about finding a publisher afterward. Because both needed to earn a living, progress on the book was slow. It took Egielski about a year to complete the art.

To their surprise, *Sid and Sol* was accepted by the second editor who saw it, Michael di Capua of Farrar, Straus & Giroux. Expecting another rejection, Yorinks had shown di Capua just the story at first and said nothing about Egielski's illustrations. But then another strange thing happened. Di Capua told Yorinks that he knew the perfect illustrator for his story—a young artist named Richard Egielski! Di Capua had seen Egielski's portfolio a year or so earlier and remembered it. To this, a dumbfounded Yorinks sputtered in reply, "But Richard already *has* illustrated the story!"

Maurice Sendak reviewed *Sid and Sol* in the *New York Times*, warmly praising the work of his talented young friends. Most reviewers, however, ignored their book about a funny little man (Sid) who somehow manages to stop an oafish giant (Sol) from destroying the world. Egielski recalls: "After *Sid and Sol*, no one knew who we were. No one ever asked for us. People didn't know we existed!" The book made very little money. While Egielski and Yorinks thought about a second book, each continued to do other work. Three years passed before they published their second picture book, *Louis the Fish*.

Yorinks had been making notes for *Louis* for over a year when late one night he wrote the whole story in nearly finished form in a single hour. Soon afterward, he stopped by Egielski's apartment with the manuscript. "I felt it was a good piece of work. Even so," Yorinks recalls,

But because his father was a
butcher and Nathan his
grand father was a butcher, he
was a butcher.
What could he do
So what he did all day
was draw fish. ~~Everywhere~~
~~On boxes.~~ On the walls.
    At first it was nothing.
A doodle here. A doodle there.
But it got worse. On boxes,
on the walls... Everywhere.
He began to have 'dreams.
One night he dreamt he was
asleep and when he woke up
he was a fish. A goldfish.
                guppy
                herring
                sardine
    It was such a happy dream.
When he got up and looked in the
mirror he was disappointed.

Arthur Yorinks's handwritten notes
for *Louis the Fish.*

"I was extremely nervous about giving it to Richard. It was such a strange story."

Egielski was feeling nervous too. "I didn't read it while he was sitting there—that would have felt like too much pressure. But I read it when he left and liked everything about it. I called Arthur right away, and from then onward it came together very quickly." Their editor, Michael di Capua, also liked the story and said he was eager to publish it.

By then Egielski and Yorinks knew exactly how they liked to work together. Bits and pieces of images, memories, and other people's stories had all found their way into Yorinks's tale about an unhappy butcher's son who daydreams about fish—and then *becomes* a fish himself. Yorinks told Egielski about these influences. The most important had been Franz Kafka's "The Metamorphosis," the surrealistic story of a young man who wakes up one morning to find that he has turned into a cockroach. Yorinks loved this powerful story that uses wild exaggeration to show how people sometimes change in ways that surprise themselves as well as everyone around them.

Not all of Yorinks's ideas came from books. The mother of a childhood friend had told him once about a relative with the very unusual habit of drawing pictures of fish on his basement walls. "That image stuck with me for years," Yorinks recalls. Before becoming a fish, Louis sits in the meat locker of the family butcher shop, drawing fish pictures.

As Egielski reread Yorinks's story, he reread Kafka's "The Metamorphosis" and thought about all the things Yorinks had told him. Pictures began to form in his mind. "I like," he says, "*not* to put anything down on paper for the first week or two. Once I put an image down, it becomes hard to forget. By running different possibilities through my head, I can decide which ones I want to remember."

Egielski next made a sequence of thumbnail sketches—squiggly pencil drawings laid out in rows like a comic strip. His goal at this stage was to show, in a general way, what each illustration would be about and how the pictures would flow from one to the next.

A few years earlier, when Egielski had first shown Yorinks his thumbnail sketches for *Sid and Sol*, Yorinks had taken one look at the artist's squiggles and thought to himself, "Uh-oh! This guy's crazy." To Yorinks, the drawings had looked like meaningless doodles. "Then I learned to read Richard's hieroglyphics. When Richard showed me the thumbnails for *Louis*, I could see they made perfect sense."

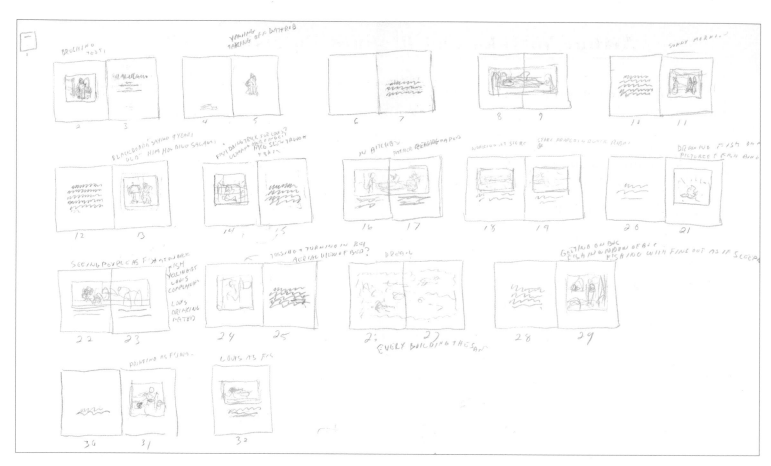

Egielski's "squiggly" thumbnail sketches.

Next Egielski made a dummy. These new drawings were highly detailed—and almost identical in composition to the finished watercolors Egielski painted in the third and final stage of his work. "*Louis* sprang up pretty much whole," he recalls with pride. "Arthur and I were really in tune."

Egielski showed his dummy, and later the first piece of finished art, to Michael di Capua, who was delighted with his progress. As work continued, Yorinks would occasionally drop by Egielski's apartment to see how things were going. The two friends often talked by phone. But as eager as Yorinks was for *Louis* to be published, he never asked Egielski when the art would be done. "I hated waiting!" Yorinks recalls.

"Arthur," says Egielski, "was very patient."

Meanwhile, their conversations—and similar backgrounds—helped Egielski to understand and picture Louis's world. "Louis's apartment is based on a friend's in the Bronx," he recalls. But the apartment might just as well have been one remembered from Yorinks's childhood. "And I got the idea of doing the aerial view of Louis

Double-page spreads from Egielski's dummy.

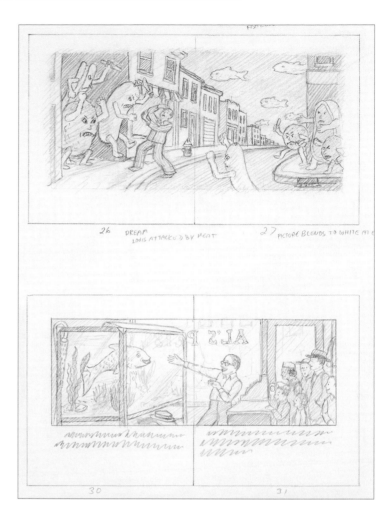

tossing and turning in bed from Alfred Hitchcock's film *Psycho*—a movie that Egielski knew Yorinks liked, too. "I thought it would add the right feeling of strangeness to the scene in which he's having his dream." And he knew that Yorinks would think so, too.

Yorinks made Louis a salmon because "the word *salmon* sounded funny to me. I'm Jewish, and because smoked salmon is a Jewish delicacy, it sort of made Louis Jewish, too, which I also thought was funny."

Egielski found his own way to have fun with the fish. "Mostly I like to make things up. But when something specific is mentioned that people might recognize, I feel I have to do a little research. When I read in Arthur's manuscript that Louis became a salmon, I thought, 'I don't know a salmon from a mackerel from a blue-fish.' And I didn't want someone who knows about fish to say, 'That doesn't look like a salmon.' So I'm thinking, 'Maybe I had better get a picture of a salmon somehow.' I remember looking around our apartment, starting with the dictionary. But there was no picture of a

Finished watercolor art by Egielski, showing Louis riding a New York City bus.

salmon there. So I went to the grocery store and I found a can of salmon. I was being very careful with my money and didn't want to buy the can. So I stripped the label off the can and put the label in my pocket and hoped I wouldn't be arrested on my way out of the store. The salmon on that can is what I used to draw Louis."

Work continued to go well. Their editor had only one major worry: what to call this very odd book. "We had a working title," Egielski says, "that I thought was great. We were going to call it 'The Butcher.' But then Michael said one day, 'That's a *horrible* title for a picture book!' So we began to think, 'What *do* you call a book like this?' We tossed around ideas. Arthur wrote out a list."

"It was Michael," Yorinks says, "who came up with 'Louis the Fish.'"

"The truth is," Egielski recalls, "we were nervous about *Louis*. It was only our second book and it was really pretty strange—with the fish and the father dying and the black bunting and all that meat! Then when *Louis* came out we got great reviews. It was thrilling to have our work recognized. We felt hopeful and optimistic. We felt kind of like a rock band!"

"People," says Yorinks, "thought of us as interchangeable. Half the time, people still didn't know who did what. But it hardly seemed to matter because now—a little bit like 'Rodgers and Hammerstein' or 'Laurel and Hardy'—we were 'Yorinks and Egielski!'"

Great reviews did not mean big sales for *Louis the Fish*, however. To their disappointment, they found that they still needed to spend much of their time doing other kinds of work. Yorinks was having some success as a playwright. Egielski illustrated for magazines, as he had done since art school. To be sure of having enough longer-term projects to keep him busy, he began to illustrate picture books by other writers as well.

Yorinks's handwritten list of possible titles.

Good things also happened for them as a team. In 1983, public television's *Reading Rainbow* featured *Louis the Fish* in its first season. *Reading Rainbow* made many more people aware of the book, which led to a jump in sales. In 1987, Egielski won the Caldecott Medal for their fourth picture-book collaboration, *Hey, Al*. After that, everyone interested in children's books knew about Yorinks and Egielski.

They did four more books together. Then, with their eighth picture book, *Christmas in July* (1991), and after more than sixteen years of working together, their collaboration seemed to come to an end.

Both say it is hard to know exactly why they stopped collaborating. According to Yorinks: "I got more involved in the theater. Richard's interest in writing his own stories grew stronger. We each started up other collaborations. But there was never one moment when we said, 'It's over.'"

According to Egielski: "*Louis* came out three years after *Sid and Sol*. *It Happened in Pinsk* came out three years after *Louis*. To keep our momentum going, we should have been doing a book a year. It hurt us that we weren't able to. I guess we were unlucky that way."

Egielski wonders whether some collaborations—like some friendships and other important relationships—simply run their course. "We knew from *Sid and Sol* that we had some things in common. That was a start. And then there's always going to be one point when collaborators are most together. For us that point came with *Louis*. But it would seem almost impossible to maintain that point for a long period of time. You can stay within a certain range of each other and continue to work together for a while, but eventually you want to do things differently. And that's when collaboration doesn't work any longer."

Both men remember the years they worked together as a good and happy time, and both say they would like one day to collaborate again. "Richard was such a master at making visual sense of my ridiculously strange stories," Yorinks recalls. "And because I could not illustrate my own picture books, it was Richard in a way who completed the stories. I could never wait to see what he would do."

The experience was much the same for Egielski: "Going from working by myself, as an art school student, to working with a collaborator was one of the greatest things that ever happened to me. It was really cool. I felt complete. With *Louis*,

Dummy layout for the final image
of a very happy Louis.

I felt that we had a really solid, seamless blending of our stuff. It was a great thing, and I think it was great for both of us."

Some Books Written by Arthur Yorinks and Illustrated by Richard Egielski

1977   *Sid and Sol* (Farrar, Straus & Giroux)

1980   *Louis the Fish* (Farrar, Straus & Giroux)

1983   *It Happened in Pinsk* (Farrar, Straus & Giroux)

1986   *Hey, Al* (Farrar, Straus & Giroux)

1988   *Bravo, Minski* (Farrar, Straus & Giroux)

1989   *Oh, Brother* (Farrar, Straus & Giroux)

1990   *Ugh* (Farrar, Straus & Giroux)

1991   *Christmas in July* (HarperCollins)

Alice Provensen

(born August 14, 1918, Chicago, Illinois)

and

Martin Provensen

(born July 10, 1916, Chicago, Illinois;
died March 27, 1987, Clinton Corners, New York)

THE GLORIOUS
FLIGHT:
Across the Channel
with Louis Blériot
(Viking, 1983)

Art medium: acrylic paints
and pen and ink

Martin and Alice Provensen,
with their dog, Muffin

Alice Provensen is reluctant, at first, to say just how she and her late husband, Martin, went about making picture books together for more than forty years. "That, of course, is the question that everybody asks. It was all very personal."

The Provensens illustrated more than forty books in all, nineteen of which they also coauthored or coedited. In none of the warmly witty, meticulously crafted books they created together is it ever obvious who did what. That is exactly as the Provensens wanted it.

Alice begins with a bit of history, explaining that it was far more common in the past for artists to collaborate than people today realize. Medieval illuminated manuscripts, for example, were the result of group efforts, the combined work of artist-monks blending their talents without concern for individual credit. In the early twentieth century, Georges Braque and Pablo Picasso did the same.

When Martin and Alice met in Los Angeles in 1943, Alice was working as an animator at the Walter Lantz Studio, creator of the Woody Woodpecker cartoons. As an animator, Alice was a member of a team of artists who produced the thousands of drawings needed to make an image appear to move on the screen. Martin, who had had a job in the story department at the rival Disney Studios before World War II, was now in the navy. He and Alice met when the navy assigned him to the Lantz Studio to help in the creation of war-related instructional films.

The Provensens' animation experience taught them the advantages of making art collaboratively. "If you weren't satisfied with a drawing and didn't know what to do next," Alice says, "the other person could help you along. Of course, it had to be the right person, one who understood what you were trying for."

In 1944, Alice and Martin married and moved east to Washington, D.C., where the couple both had war-related jobs. After peace was declared, in August 1945, they moved to New York, where an artist friend, Gustaf Tenggren, helped them find their first assignments as book illustrators. From then on, the Provensens always worked as a team.

In some ways, Alice and Martin had led parallel lives in the years before they met. Both were born in Chicago to parents who encouraged their interest in art. As children, both had read a great deal and delighted in the traveling "air circuses"—daredevil flying exhibitions performed out in the countryside—that were a popular midwestern form of entertainment in the early days of commercial aviation. Both were largely self-trained artists by the time they met in Los Angeles.

In 1950, the Provensens bought an abandoned farm north of New York City and set up their studio in a converted barn a few steps from their house.

The couple worked at large drawing tables placed back-to-back in the barn. Privacy was

The Provensens' barn/studio
at Maple Hill Farm.

rarely a concern. "Once in a while one of us may have had an idea we were just developing that we didn't want the other person to see just yet." When that happened, Alice recalls, "we would string a curtain up between our desks. But we did that only occasionally."

Martin made lunch; Alice cooked dinner. Martin did the outdoor work; Alice did the housework and bookkeeping. Both looked after their daughter, Karen, who was born in 1958.

For fun, Alice liked to rebind old books, while Martin forged paintings by old and modern masters. The "Rembrandts," "Picassos," and other world-famous art on view throughout their house were all actually Martin's handiwork. Martin loved to watch for the look of bewilderment of first-time visitors as it dawned on them to wonder how their hosts could possibly own so many masterpieces. From childhood onward, Martin also loved to build model airplanes.

The Provensens had illustrated more than thirty books, most of them for children, when they decided to make a picture book inspired by their shared lifelong fascination with flight. At first the couple knew only that they wanted to tell a story from aviation history. After doing some research, they found themselves drawn to the bold exploits of a French inventor and aviation pioneer named Louis Blériot. It was Blériot who in 1909 had become the first person to fly solo across the English Channel—an amazing feat for the time. Compared with the Wright brothers' earlier history-making (but far shorter) flight, Blériot's glorious achievement was little known to Americans. The Provensens liked the idea of telling a story that would be new to many of their readers.

The couple found very little about Blériot in American libraries, and this made them even more curious about their subject. A friend sent research materials from France. But the Provensens did find other help—and inspiration—from a source close to home.

In the late 1950s, to Alice and Martin's delight, an antique airplane museum and flying school called the Old Rhinebeck Aerodrome had opened in a town not far from their farm. Alice and Martin enjoyed attending the weekend air shows put on by the owner and staff. By the time the couple had begun work on *The Glorious Flight*, Martin was also taking flying lessons there.

The museum's plane collection included three original Blériot XI biplanes, the

A dummy spread, with added bits of dialogue in French.

same type of aircraft flown in the historic 1909 Channel crossing. Fledgling pilots such as Martin were not permitted to fly the fragile, lightweight Blériots, which looked to Alice like "bundles of sticks with sewing-machine engines." Just seeing the flimsy planes up close, however, made a deep impression on both collaborators. Examining the planes brought home to them an awareness of the great danger that Blériot had so willingly faced. Blériot's bravery, and "the fact that he did it alone," Alice recalls, is what made his story seem worth telling.

The manuscript came first. "We wanted the text to have a sort of oddball quality," she says. "We tried to tell the story 'with a French accent.'" Occasional changes in standard word order ("Out of the clouds, right over their heads, soars a great white airship"), and the use of a few French and French-sounding words ("café," "aeronaut") helped to create this playful impression.

They then designed the format and prepared the dummy they showed their editor at The Viking Press, Linda Zuckerman. Martin drew the dummy in the cartoon style he had used at the Disney Studios, years earlier, to sketch out the general outlines of an animation story. He had fun as he worked, writing in extra bits of amusing dialogue, in French, over the heads of Blériot and his companions: *"Tiens!"* ("Hold on!") and *"Mauvais chance . . ."* ("Bad luck . . ."). The Provensens later decided not to keep these additional French words or the design element of cartoon balloon-style dialogue.

Linda Zuckerman looked over the dummy and told the artists to go ahead,

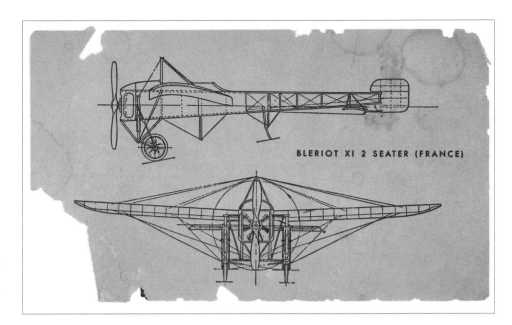

Page clipped by the Provensens from an unidentified source as research material for *The Glorious Flight.*

Double-page spread from Martin Provensen's dummy showing earlier versions of the inventor's plane.

trusting from long experience that Alice and Martin would know what to do next. They proceeded to make dozens and dozens of sketches, which they posted on their studio walls as they searched for the illustration style that best suited their text. As they continued to experiment, they consulted the sketchbooks they had kept, years earlier, while traveling in France. The drawings and paintings in those sketchbooks provided all the research material they needed for the French street scenes and landscapes of their illustrations.

Gouache study from the Provensens'
travel sketchbook, 1959.

The art for *The Glorious Flight* changed dramatically from the wiry slapstick drawings of Martin's original dummy to the more formal—but still quite droll—finished paintings that he and Alice produced together. Nonetheless, Alice recalls this part of the work as having gone very smoothly. "We were confident," she says. "When you have a story and a dummy that's that strong, you know what to do."

Once they had agreed on a style for the art, Alice and Martin informally—and without ever having to talk about it—divided up some of the tasks that lay ahead. Martin painted most of the portraits of Blériot. Alice did most of the hand-lettering for the book jacket and title page and for the old-fashioned contest poster that inspired Blériot to build his plane.

"We both worked on most of the drawings and paintings," Alice recalls, "sometimes with one of us doing the background and the other doing the costumes and figures."

In Martin's dummy sketch for the illustration showing Blériot in flight soon after takeoff, numerous details of the scene on the ground are highlighted. In the finished painting, however, all but the airplane hangar have been eliminated. "We did this to emphasize just how very alone he was up there," Alice explains. In every scene in which the Frenchman appears, whether painted by Alice or Martin, Blériot's eyes are set with a look of fearless determination. As always, the Provensens took their time. They completed *The Glorious Flight* in about one year.

Alice's studio copy of *The Glorious Flight* bears an inscription, written in French, that translates as: "For the Provensens—Alice and Martin—with my sincere good wishes, Louis Blériot."

"That," says Alice, "was Martin's work, of course."

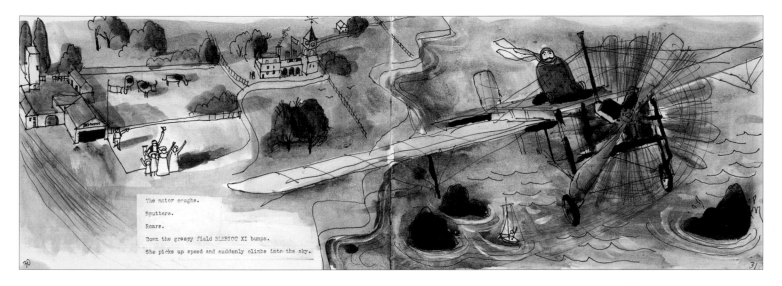

Martin Provensen's dummy illustration for the scene depicting Blériot's historic ascent. In the finished illustration for this scene, nearly all the background detail has been eliminated.

When Martin Provensen died of a heart attack in 1987, at the age of seventy, Alice was unsure whether she would ever be able to work again. A period of terrible uncertainty followed, during which the couple's editor, Linda Zuckerman, urged her to try. Alice's love of research finally came to her aid. She immersed herself in work on a large picture book about the presidents of the United States, called *The Buck Stops Here* (1990). Alice took the title from the sign that President Harry S Truman kept on his desk in the Oval Office, as a statement of his sense of ultimate responsibility as the nation's leader. In her own way, Alice, too, was taking complete charge of matters. After Martin died, she had considered selling Maple Hill Farm. When *The Buck Stops Here* proved to be a critical and commercial success, Alice changed her mind and built an addition to a house that, Alice says, "already seemed too big."

Perhaps one reason for the success of the Provensens' collaboration was that their likes and dislikes so often complemented one another. Martin, for instance, never enjoyed speaking in public, while Alice has generally felt quite comfortable before an audience. Alice has never been eager to have her voice recorded, whereas Martin felt fine about being taped. When the couple won the Caldecott Medal in 1984 for *The Glorious Flight,* it was Alice who delivered their acceptance speech at the award ceremony attended by hundreds of librarians and publishers. And it was Martin

This is more like it. Here is «BLÉRIOT II,» a glider. Big enough to hold a man.
Papa has not yet learned to pilot, so Gabriel Voisin, his good friend, will fly.

A motorboat will tow it into the air as the glider has no motor.
All is in readiness. Gabriel gives the signal.

Finished art and text by Alice and Martin Provensen from *The Glorious Flight*.

whose voice was heard on the tape-recorded version of the speech that was given as a keepsake to those present. "So it all worked out very well," says Alice.

Alice cannot recall how she and Martin went about writing their speech. The question seems unimportant to her. "You see," she says at last, "we were a true collaboration. Martin and I really were one artist."

Some Books by Alice and Martin Provensen

1947	*The Fireside Book of Folksongs* (text edited by Margaret Bradford Boni; Simon & Schuster)
1949	*The Color Kittens* (text by Margaret Wise Brown; Golden Press)
1956	*Iliad and Odyssey* (text adapted by Jane Werner Watson; Golden Press)
1964	*The Charge of the Light Brigade* (text by Alfred Lord Tennyson; Golden Press)

1976   *A Book of Seasons* (Random House)

1976   *The Mother Goose Book* (Random House)

1978   *The Year at Maple Hill Farm* (Atheneum)

1978   *A Peaceable Kingdom: The Shaker Abecedarius* (Viking)

1981   *A Visit to William Blake's Inn: Poems for Innocent and Experienced Travelers* (text by Nancy Willard; Harcourt)

1982   *Birds, Beasts, and the Third Thing: Poems* (text by D. H. Lawrence; Viking)

1983   *The Glorious Flight: Across the Channel with Louis Blériot* (Viking)

1984   *Town and Country* (Crown)

1987   *The Voyage of the Ludgate Hill: Travels with Robert Louis Stevenson* (text by Nancy Willard; Harcourt)

1987   *Shaker Lane* (Viking)

Jon Scieszka,

(born September 8, 1954, Flint, Michigan)

Lane Smith,

(born August 25, 1959, Tulsa, Oklahoma)

and

Molly Leach

(born October 4, 1960, Champaign, Illinois)

Lane Smith (left) and
Jon Scieszka

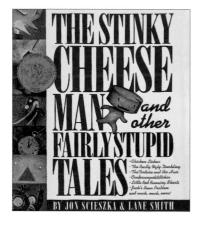

*THE STINKY CHEESE MAN
AND OTHER FAIRLY
STUPID TALES*
(Viking, 1992)

Art medium:
oil on paper

Molly Leach

Growing up as the second of six brothers, Jon Scieszka learned early on about collaboration—and getting along. The Scieszkas lived in Flint, Michigan, where Jon's father was a school principal and his mother was a nurse. He and his older brother, Jim, teamed up to build go-carts, play toy soldiers, and hurl dirt clods at the neighbors. In their busy household, it was often the two elder brothers' job to baby-sit the little "knuckleheads."

Jon liked to read as a child. Inspired by one of his favorite authors, Dr. Seuss, he also wrote poems and stories and sometimes imagined himself an author. At school, science classes held special interest for him, and for a time Jon thought about becoming a doctor. He never forgot his dream of a writing career, however, and when, following college, he moved to New York in 1978, he did so with the goal of becoming a fiction writer for adults and possibly also an English professor.

In New York, Scieszka enrolled in writing classes at Columbia University. About a year later, he got married. To make money, Scieszka painted apartments and then took a job as a teacher in a Manhattan school. He found that he loved to teach. He enjoyed his second-graders' sense of fun and admired their eagerness to try new things. Then, after three years of teaching, and of having no luck at publishing his adult short stories, Scieszka decided to try something new. Taking a year's leave of absence from his job, he worked at home on a new batch of stories—this time, stories for children.

The first several publishers to whom he sent these new stories turned them down. Then Scieszka's wife, Jeri Hansen, who was an art director at *Sport* magazine, introduced him to an illustrator she recently had met at work.

Lane Smith, an Oklahoma-born artist with a busy freelance career, had been hired by *Sport* to do an illustration showing a name-brand sneaker taking a bite out of a rival company's shoe. Scieszka, who disliked the "fuzzy-bunny pastel picture-

Oil illustration by Lane Smith for the April 1986 issue of *Travel and Leisure* magazine, for an article about Costa Rican wildlife.

book world" of the children's books he usually saw in stores, was fascinated by Smith's sly, shadowy illustrations, which he found "so funny and weird." The two men's first outing together, a trip to the Bronx Zoo, went awkwardly, with Smith trying repeatedly to start up a "serious" conversation and Scieszka responding with knock-knock jokes.

"I thought, 'What's with this guy?'" Smith recalls. They both may have been a bit nervous. They soon realized, however, that they shared a similar sense of humor and a great many interests. As children they had both loved Ruth Krauss and Crockett Johnson's *The Carrot Seed* as well as Dr. Seuss books, *Mad* magazine, and Warner Brothers cartoons like the one in which Bugs Bunny comes along with a giant eraser and rubs out one of the other characters. Soon they began to talk about collaborating on a book.

It had been Jeri Hansen's friend and fellow art director at *Sport*, Molly Leach, who hired Smith for the sneaker assignment; not long after they met, Smith and Leach began to go out together. Now the two couples saw each other often.

Although Smith worked primarily for magazines, he had already illustrated three picture books—*Halloween ABC* (1987) by Eve Merriam, his own *Flying Jake* (1988), and the then still unpublished *Glasses—Who Needs 'Em?* (1991)—and was eager to do more. Now, when Smith showed his artwork to publishers, he brought along Scieszka's stories. As had happened before, the first editors to whom Smith showed the stories failed to see the humor in them. Finally, however, an editor at Viking Penguin, Regina Hayes, laughed out loud as she read through the stories and said she wanted to publish one of them, with illustrations by Smith. *The True Story of the 3 Little Pigs!* (1989) proved to be very popular.

It was so popular, in fact, that the two friends were soon being invited to speak at schools all around the United States. Scieszka enjoyed putting on these shows for schoolchildren. Smith, however, who was used to the privacy of his studio, felt shy at first about performing for an audience.

The main problem the pair faced was that it took just a few minutes to read their one and only collaborative picture book aloud. Smith made easel drawings for the children, which filled up some time. They both answered questions. Even so, it was clear they needed more material.

In desperation, Scieszka dusted off a folder of fairy-tale parodies he had written

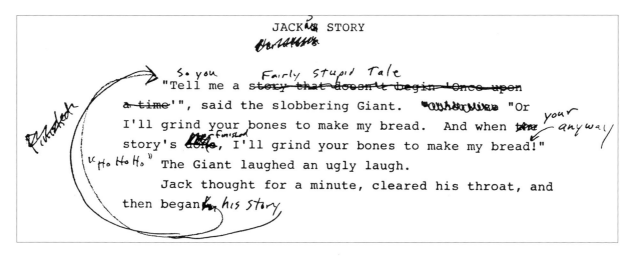

Manuscript page with handwritten revisions by Scieszka for "Jack's Story."

over the past few years and filed away as unpublishable. "See, kids," he'd say as he began to read from the folder, "not everything a writer does works out!" He had written one of the stories, "The Stinky Cheese Man," to amuse himself after having read the classic tale on which it was based—"The Gingerbread Boy"—so often to his daughter at bedtime that he could no longer bear to hear the original version!

The youngest schoolchildren he and Smith met were not used to such odd stories and often were unsure when Scieszka had finished reading. Because of this, he began to make a point, when the time came, of announcing in a big voice: "The End." The children found this joke—and much else about his "fairly stupid tales"—hilarious, so much so that he and Smith began to talk about making a book of the stories.

Scieszka kept fiddling with the stories. He would ask himself: "Should it be 'The Really Stupid Duckling' or 'The Really Really Ugly Duckling'?" Often when he performed a story for a group of children, he would change a word or two to see whether the new version prompted a stronger audience response. Finally, after making a number of such small changes, he felt ready to give copies of the stories to Smith and to Viking Penguin editor Regina Hayes.

Smith made a list of the tales he could readily imagine illustrating. "With 'The Really Ugly Duckling' and 'The Stinky Cheese Man,'" he recalls, "I thought, 'Oh, that's funny. That's *great*.' But when I first read 'Cinderrumpelstiltskin,' I told myself, 'I'll get to that one later.'"

Hayes made a list of the stories she found funniest. She knew right away that

"The Stinky Cheese Man" would make a memorable title for the collection.

As they tried to imagine their new book, Scieszka and Smith became intrigued with the idea of poking fun not only at fairy tales but also at books in general. "I knew that second-graders would get a kick out of a book that broke lots of rules," Scieszka says, "because they're a group that has just found out that there *are* rules—such as where the title page belongs." Scieszka made lists of all the book-related pranks he could think of. He and Smith traded ideas, often over a game of Ping-Pong at the artist's Manhattan studio.

What if the table of contents was a big mess, and did not appear, as expected, at the start of the book? What if a page was left completely blank and the text of another page printed upside down? What if characters from one story wandered, as though lost, from one story to another? These and other ideas later found their way into the design and illustration of *The Stinky Cheese Man*.

With the text in nearly finished form, Smith made his first sketches. Scieszka, who could not quite visualize the "little man of cheese" or any of his other characters, was eager to see how Smith would depict them. Of this stage of the work, Scieszka recalls: "I never considered saying to Lane, 'Could you make the fox's tail a little bushier?' That kind of thing just drives illustrators crazy! I knew my job at that point was to cheer Lane on." As work progressed, Scieszka visited Smith's studio nearly every day.

For most children's books, the basic design work—the choice of type, for example, and often the choice of the cover image—is done by a member of the publisher's staff. But Scieszka and Smith knew that *The Stinky Cheese Man* would be funny only if every bit of the design helped to advance their goal of making a storybook in which nothing happened as expected. Because *The True Story of the 3 Little Pigs!* had been a best-seller—more than 250,000 copies were sold in the first year—Viking Penguin agreed to let the pair choose their own designer for *The Stinky Cheese Man*. They chose Molly Leach.

Leach, whose studio was one flight up in the same loft building as Smith's, now became a full member of the team. "My job," Leach says, "was to be the problem-solver. Lane or Jon would have some funny idea. I had to make it fit within the book as a whole."

Smith offers this example: "For 'Jack's Story,' which repeats itself endlessly, I originally imagined having the text set as a circle of type, going around and around. But in good design, nothing should stand out too much, and Molly pointed out

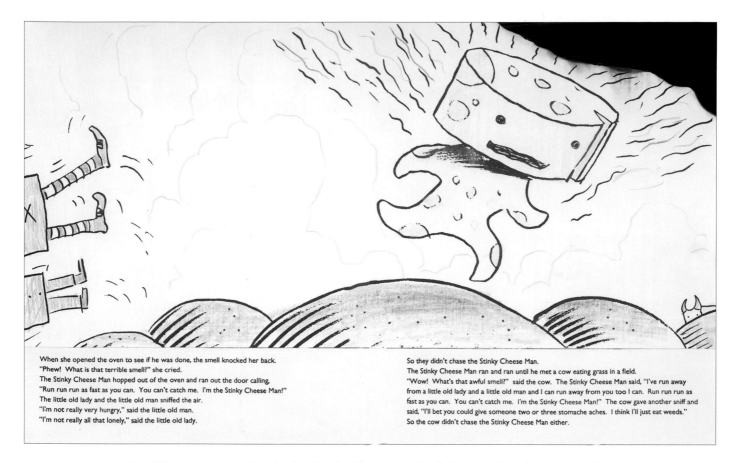

When she opened the oven to see if he was done, the smell knocked her back.
"Phew! What is that terrible smell?" she cried.
The Stinky Cheese Man hopped out of the oven and ran out the door calling,
"Run run run as fast as you can. You can't catch me. I'm the Stinky Cheese Man!"
The little old lady and the little old man sniffed the air.
"I'm not really very hungry," said the little old man.
"I'm not really all that lonely," said the little old lady.

So they didn't chase the Stinky Cheese Man.
The Stinky Cheese Man ran and ran until he met a cow eating grass in a field.
"Wow! What's that awful smell?" said the cow. The Stinky Cheese Man said, "I've run away from a little old lady and a little old man and I can run away from you too I can. Run run run as fast as you can. You can't catch me. I'm the Stinky Cheese Man!" The cow gave another sniff and said, "I'll bet you could give someone two or three stomache aches. I think I'll just eat weeds." So the cow didn't chase the Stinky Cheese Man either.

Double-page spread with the "melted" corner for "The Stinky Cheese Man" story, from the dummy prepared by Smith and Leach.

that a circle shape would be unlike any other arrangement of type in the book. So we nixed the circle and went with Molly's idea of having the type get smaller and smaller down the page."

Smith describes Leach's role this way: "Jon and I both appreciate goofy, second-grade humor. If it were up to us, we would use all comic-book type or hand-lettered type made of twigs. Molly, with her background in magazine design, is different. She'll take what we do—and make it classy." Leach and Smith had something important in common, too. Because they both had worked for magazines, they were used to solving design problems rapidly, and to meeting deadlines.

Together, Smith and Leach made a book dummy and, after discussing it with Scieszka, presented their work to Regina Hayes. Hayes, while delighted overall, zeroed in on certain problems in the design, including some that she knew would add greatly to the cost of printing. For the scene where the Stinky Cheese Man is melting in the oven, for example, Smith and Leach had torn off the upper corner

The Stinky Cheese Man ran and ran until he met some kids playing outside school.
"Gross," said a little girl. "What's that nasty smell?"
"I've run away from a little old lady, and a little old man, and a cow, and I can run away from you too I can. Run run run as fast as you can. You can't catch me.

I'm the Stinky Cheese Man!"
A little boy looked up, sniffed the air and said, "If we catch him, our teacher will probably make us eat him. Let's get out of here."
So the kids didn't chase the Stinky Cheese Man either.

Reverse side of the dummy spread featuring a "melted" page corner.

of the page as a way of suggesting that the paper itself had melted from the heat. Hayes saw the humor in the idea but said it would "cost a million dollars" to reproduce the torn-paper "special effect" in a picture book. As an alternative, Leach hand-lettered the type at the top of the page, making it appear to droop as though wilting from the heat of the oven.

Leach liked bold, headline-sized type like that often used for magazines. She thought that unusually big, dramatic type best communicated the fun of stories in which things continually went haywire. And she wanted each page to feel as if it were ready to burst at the margins. Hayes liked Leach's idea but persuaded her to leave *some* space around the text for the reader's eye to rest.

After offering her comments, Hayes gave the collaborators her blessing. The next time she met with them was to see Smith's finished art laid out in Leach's completed design.

Meanwhile, *The Stinky Cheese Man* continued to change. Hayes had urged the trio to keep to a fifty-six-page limit (nearly twice as long as a standard thirty-two-page picture book). Then one day, after thinking the book was almost done, the three collaborators suddenly realized that they had way too much material—that *The Stinky Cheese Man* had become much too long a book. "That," Smith recalls, "is when the *real* collaboration began."

At Leach's suggestion, Smith redid some paintings to make more space for Scieszka's words. Scieszka shortened "Jack's Bean Problem" to leave more room for the illustration of the giant's shoe.

Now Scieszka made another list, this time grouping the stories according to the reason each was funny. "The Tortoise and the Hair," for instance, was humorous because it had no real ending. The Little Red Hen's story was funny because none of the other characters mentioned in it ever actually showed up. Thinking about the manuscript in this way helped the team eliminate stories that repeated the same joke.

From first sketches to final layouts and paintings, the illustrations and design of

Finished double-page spread featuring the Little Red Hen,
the Giant, and Leach's unique type treatment.

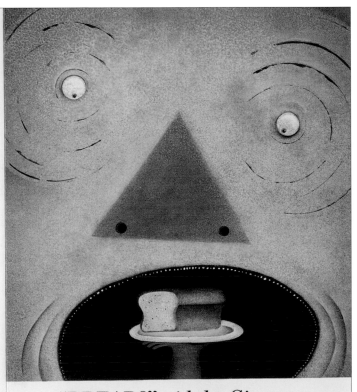

"I found the wheat.
I planted the wheat. I grew
the wheat. I harvested the
wheat. I ground the wheat.
I made the dough. I baked
the bread," said the Little
Red Hen. "And did anyone
help me? Did anyone
save space for my story?
So now," said the Little
Red Hen, "who
thinks they're
going to help
me EAT the
BREAD?"

"BREAD?" said the Giant.
"EAT?" said the Giant.

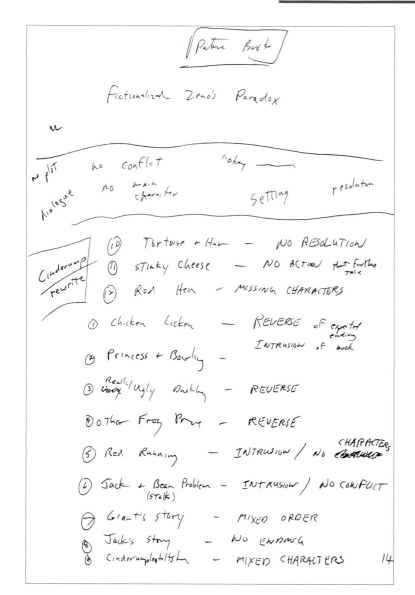

Handwritten list by Scieszka pinpointing each story's main comic element.

The Stinky Cheese Man came together rapidly, in about two months of intensive effort. At her drafting table late one evening, Leach cut her finger—but kept on working! She was determined to finish her first book assignment on time.

Viking Penguin published *The Stinky Cheese Man* on schedule in the fall of 1992. The book proved to be extraordinarily popular, even more so than *The True Story of the 3 Little Pigs!* Second-graders, the readers Scieszka originally had in mind, reveled in it, in part because it made them feel a bit grown up. Eighth-graders also liked it, and so did many readers of the grades in between. Adults bought copies of the book for their own amusement, too.

Reviewers praised *The Stinky Cheese Man* as not only an entertaining book but also an original one in spirit and design. Teachers and librarians agreed. Much to the surprise of Scieszka, Smith, and Leach, who knew how unconventional their book was, in 1993 *The Stinky Cheese Man* was awarded a Caldecott Honor—the second-highest illustration prize (after the Caldecott Medal) that can be given to an American picture book.

Not everyone "got" *The Stinky Cheese Man.* As one of the book's many gags, the dedication page was printed upside down. Scieszka says, "We still receive letters about this from people complaining that there is something wrong with their copy."

Designers do not ordinarily receive equal credit alongside the author and illustrator of a book. In *The Stinky Cheese Man*, Molly Leach's name appears only once—in the fine print on the copyright page. Leach says she has never been bothered by this and is pleased that her contribution to the book was given an unusual amount of attention by critics. According to Scieszka: "People leafing through *The Stinky Cheese Man* would see that something different was going on—and realize that a good part of that 'something' was Molly's design." Other picture books began to have explosions of bold type placed at odd angles or in wavy lines. Writers and illustrators began to imitate Scieszka and Smith as well.

What made *The Stinky Cheese Man* special to so many people? Scieszka says: "People would call our book 'wacky,' 'zany,' 'anything-goes' kind of fun. When I look back, though, I think, 'Not really.' It was actually very carefully planned. Doing humor is like ditch digging! You do it over and over again until you get to the bottom of the thing. What kept us going—the question we always asked ourselves—was: How do we get the biggest possible laugh? How do we make the best possible book?"

"We were just happy," adds Smith, "they let us get away with it!"

Some Books Written by Jon Scieszka, Illustrated by Lane Smith, and Designed by Molly Leach

1992   *The Stinky Cheese Man and Other Fairly Stupid Tales* (Viking)

1995   *Math Curse* (Viking)

1998   *Squids Will Be Squids: Fresh Morals, Beastly Fables* (Viking)

2001   *Baloney (Henry P.)* (Viking)

Julius Lester

(born January 27, 1939, St. Louis, Missouri)

and

Jerry Pinkney

(born December 22, 1939, Philadelphia, Pennsylvania)

Julius Lester

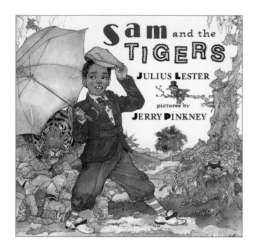

SAM AND THE TIGERS:
A New Telling
of Little Black Sambo
(Dial, 1996)

Art medium:
pencil and
watercolor

Jerry Pinkney

Sometimes good friends become collaborators. Other times, after years of publishing their work side by side, collaborators become good friends. It happened that way for artist Jerry Pinkney and writer Julius Lester.

Long before they met, Lester and Pinkney shared an editor, Phyllis Fogelman of Dial Books for Young Readers. Fogelman had published many books by each man when Lester brought his "The Tales of Uncle Remus" to her. When Fogelman suggested Jerry Pinkney as the book's illustrator, the author agreed that Pinkney had just the right style for depicting the fanciful blend of animal and human characters found in the old stories. Pinkney, who had admired Lester's adult fiction for years, felt honored to be chosen as his collaborator.

As busy, seasoned professionals living in small towns hundreds of miles apart, Lester and Pinkney saw no need to get together to discuss the progress of their book.

During this time, Lester did happen to meet Pinkney, and his wife, Gloria Jean, at a library convention. And Lester saw the artist's Uncle Remus illustrations as they came in at their publisher's office and offered an occasional suggestion through their editor. *The Tales of Uncle Remus* was published in 1987 to general praise.

A Brer Rabbit sequel, *More Tales of Uncle Remus,* appeared in 1988, followed two years later by a second sequel, *Further Tales of Uncle Remus* (1990)*. Lester's and Pinkney's paths continued to cross occasionally. But although the two collaborators now considered themselves friends, they still had not met for a work session.

They had their first long work-related conversation—over the telephone—in 1993, after Pinkney proposed a picture book to Fogelman based on the legend of John Henry. The artist and editor both hoped that Lester would write the text, but Lester, who had never thought of John Henry as one of his heroes, needed persuading. As the two men talked, Lester began to see John Henry differently, as a larger-than-life figure resembling Dr. Martin Luther King Jr. Pinkney's words had led him in this direction. "That," Lester recalls, "is when we *really* started collaborating." *John Henry* won numerous awards, including a 1995 Caldecott Honor.

One day while Pinkney was making preliminary drawings for what he and Lester assumed would be their next collaboration—a picture book about the American West called *Black Cowboy, Wild Horses* (1997)—Lester called to say that he would soon be traveling near Pinkney's upstate New York home and wondered if he might stop by. Pinkney had recently told Lester that he was having trouble dividing the text into a series of visually dramatic scenes. Lester was not sure what he could do to help the illustrator, but he was eager to try. He brought along his laptop, thinking that he might do some rewriting that very afternoon. Lester recalls that as the two men talked, he began for the first time to understand the picture book as an art form in which the action unfolds bit by bit, with each turn of the page. They enjoyed the easy give-and-take of their conversation. Each recognized in the other a craftsman ready to make any change needed for the sake of their book. That day, both men felt that their friendship deepened.

Then, not long afterward, Lester read a message on the Internet that changed their plans. The message concerned one of literature's most controversial books, a century-old children's picture book by Helen Bannerman called *The Story of Little Black Sambo* (1899).

---

* A third sequel, *The Last Tales of Uncle Remus,* was published in 1994.

Bannerman was a Scottish woman living in India at the time she wrote and illustrated *The Story of Little Black Sambo* for the amusement of her two young daughters. Bannerman was as surprised as anybody when her little fantasy about a boy who outwits a band of tigers became a best-seller on both sides of the Atlantic.

The book first caused a stir in the 1930s, when librarians objected to Bannerman's depiction of Sambo and his family as dark-skinned folk with big lips, bulging eyes, and other exaggerated features. These librarians, unlike those of Bannerman's generation, saw the drawings as an insult to people of color.

Not everyone took Bannerman's book in the same way, however. Growing up in a comfortable African-American neighborhood in Philadelphia during the 1940s, Jerry Pinkney had felt a certain fondness for *The Story of Little Black Sambo*. The book had appealed to him as one of the few children's books he knew that included people of color. And he had enjoyed the fantasy of a boy able to outsmart

Illustrations from *The Story of Little Black Sambo* (1899),
written and illustrated by Helen Bannerman.

tigers. As a child, Pinkney himself had rarely experienced racial prejudice firsthand. His family owned a copy of Bannerman's book, and the artist feels today that his parents never would have allowed it in their home had they considered the book offensive.

Pinkney went on to attend art school, launch a career as a commercial artist, and take part in the Civil Rights movement of the 1960s. During the 1980s, he turned increasingly to illustrating children's books, the majority of them on African-American themes. In all that time, he thought little about Bannerman's book.

Then, one day in 1994 or 1995, during a research visit to the Charles Brockson Afro-American Collection at Philadelphia's Temple University, he learned that as many as fifty artists had come along after Helen Bannerman and published their own reillustrated versions of the Sambo story. Like Bannerman, these artists had exaggerated the characters' racial features. While no one knows for sure why Bannerman depicted her characters in that way, we do know that many of the later artists intentionally drew their caricatures to fuel racial hatred. "Seeing these versions," Pinkney recalls, "was the spark. I realized that if they could do their versions of the story, I could do mine—and right the wrongs" of the earlier books.

To do this, however, Pinkney first had to find his own way of telling the story. He began by studying the older versions and talking about the Bannerman book with librarians and others who remembered it from childhood. Now, whenever he spoke in public, he mentioned *The Story of Little Black Sambo*, hoping to draw out his listeners' memories and to test the reaction that a new retelling might cause.

Then one day while reading his E-mail, Julius Lester came across a message that surprised him. The note, posted by a member of a children's-literature discussion group he belonged to, reported that Jerry Pinkney was at work on a new version of *The Story of Little Black Sambo*.

The news was of more than passing interest to Lester. Like Pinkney, Lester had strong childhood memories of *Sambo*. As a boy, he had enjoyed imagining tigers turned to butter and the huge stack of pancakes that was the small child's reward. But unlike Pinkney, Lester had grown up as a minister's son in the segregated South. It had seemed obvious to him early on that Bannerman's illustrations were racist caricatures, images meant to make black people look—and feel—inferior to whites. As an adult,

Instead they ran faster and faster around the tree until
all Sam could see was a blur! Faster and faster and faster and
faster the Tigers went until ----- they melted! That's right! The
anger got the tigers going so fast that they melted away.

Double-page spread from Pinkney's dummy for the scene in which the tigers turn to butter.

Lester studied the history of racial bigotry and was aware that, over the years, Bannerman's book had often been used to reinforce hateful stereotypes; that the name "Sambo" had become a slur used by white racists against men of color.

Lester also knew that during the Civil Rights movement, the book had been banned from libraries for this very reason. This fact made the history of Bannerman's story still more complicated—and interesting—for him. In the 1960s Lester himself had thought it right to urge that a copy of *The Story of Little Black Sambo* be removed from the shelves of his local library. Now, thirty years later, he felt troubled by the thought of any book being kept out of readers' hands. In recent months, Lester had taken part in two lively Internet discussions about Bannerman's book and been "struck by the fact that . . . [so] many people retained fond memories of [it] even while knowing now that the characters were depicted in an offensive way."

When Lester read the message about Jerry Pinkney, he immediately telephoned the artist. "I understand you're working on a retelling," Lester began. Amused to realize that his comments to librarians had launched a rumor in cyberspace,

Pinkney replied with a laugh, "Well, I've been *thinking* about it."

Lester was not sure what to think. Why had the artist not mentioned any of this to him a few months earlier, on the day they had met? With mock outrage, he pressed the issue: "How dare you think about a project like that without asking me to be involved!" Then, softening his voice, he got to the real point. "I have an interest myself. . . .Would you like to collaborate?"

There was a long pause at the other end of the line. Pinkney had become convinced that a new retelling was bound to be controversial. He really had not made up his mind whether to go ahead.

"Why not?" he heard himself telling his friend at last. "Let's give it a shot."

Lester promised to send him a manuscript in two weeks' time.

Meanwhile, Pinkney continued to have his worries. "I would wake up in the middle of the night thinking, '*What a great idea!*' then wake up the next night wondering, 'Is this *really* what I want to be doing?'" Pinkney worried that critics would see a new version—even one that had been created by historically aware African Americans—as keeping alive a book that had long given aid and comfort to hate mongers. He was unsure whether he wanted to fight that battle. Some nights, he hoped the manuscript would never arrive.

As Lester prepared to write the promised first draft, he too was feeling "pretty terrified, knowing how people felt" about *The Story of Little Black Sambo.* "The big problem was the name—Sambo. I wanted a name for the hero that would be similar to the one in Bannerman's story, but not offensive. I didn't know what to do about the name. Then one morning I was lying in bed, saying the name 'Sam' over to myself, and suddenly came up with 'Sam-sam-sa-mara.' I liked that as a name for the setting. I then thought, 'Why not name *everyone* in the story Sam?' I laughed at the thought, got out of bed, went to the computer, and wrote the first draft."

Having found his foothold in Bannerman's tale, Lester resolved to make the story his own in other ways, too. To highlight the fantasy element—the aspect of the story he had loved as a child—he introduced more talking animals, including Miss Cat from whom young Sam buys his yellow shirt. "Then I brought in Brer Rabbit as a way of rooting it in the black storytelling tradition." He changed Bannerman's tale about a child who receives a new set of clothes into a coming-of-age story in which the young hero chooses new clothes for himself as a sign of his growing independence.

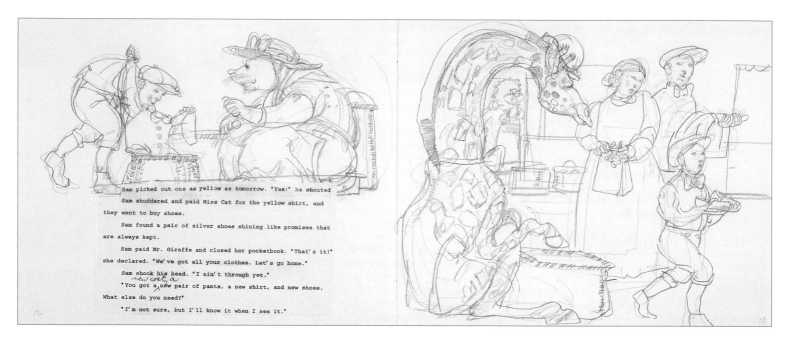

Double-page spread from Pinkney's dummy, featuring Sam, Miss Cat, and Mr. Giraffe.

Lester, who admired Bannerman's skill as a storyteller, recalls: "I found that her text was a model of directness and simplicity—and that there was nothing I could do to improve on the way she wrote it. So I decided that to justify a new version I would have to go in the opposite direction—toward a more poetic and lyrical style of language."

Jerry Pinkney was still having his worries when, as promised, Lester's manuscript arrived in the mail. "I read it," the artist recalls, "and breathed a sigh of relief because I knew it was wonderful."

It was now time to talk with Phyllis Fogelman. The editor reacted much as the two men had: with alarm followed by a sense of excitement. Predicting that the book would get lots of attention, she urged them to set aside *Black Cowboy, Wild Horses* and do *Sam and the Tigers* first. They agreed to this plan. While Lester continued to tinker with the manuscript, Pinkney made a series of thumbnail sketches and then a more detailed dummy. In a sign of their growing mutual trust, Pinkney sent Lester copies of these early drawings. "It was the first time," he recalls, "that I shared this part of the process with an author."

BRIGHT SUN
NEED UMBRELLA

A sequence of Pinkney's thumbnail sketches.

As Pinkney drew, he felt guided by the power of Lester's words. The playfulness and flamboyance of the text brought to mind the bold style of dress Pinkney had admired in photographic portraits of African Americans taken in the segregated rural South of the 1920s. Pinkney had pored over books of such photographs, fascinated by the evident dignity and strength of people living under conditions of terrible prejudice and hardship. Pinkney saw young Sam as embodying the same qualities. Inspired by the photos, he set *Sam and the Tigers* in a 1920s southern town. He

posed and photographed his grandson, Myles, as his model for Sam. These new photos, together with the old ones, helped Pinkney as he refined his increasingly detailed drawings.

Pinkney also felt guided by his conversations with Lester about the latter's childhood in the South of the 1940s. Lester had recalled, for example, driving to Arkansas to visit his grandmother, seeing Arkansas license plates, which bore the motto "Land of Opportunity," and "understanding that that did not include me." Hearing such true stories deepened Pinkney's feeling for the tale about brave and quick-witted Sam.

Lester no longer thought to offer Pinkney advice, as he had on earlier books. Writing rapidly, he continued

Reference photo by Jerry Pinkney of his grandson, Myles, posing as Sam.

Dummy sketch by Pinkney.

Back in the times when animals and people were still on speaking terms there lived a little boy named Sam.

Sam lived in Samsamsamara. Don't come asking me where it was because I don't rightly know. It could have been on the outskirts of Philly-Me-York. Then, again it probably wasn't no place except inside somebody's brain and after I finish with the story, it'll be in your brain, too.

Sam's mama was named Sam. Sam's daddy was named Sam. In fact, everybody in Samsamsamara was named Sam. You might think that would make things confusing.

SAM AND THE TIGERS: FOURTH DRAFT (7/24/95)

Once upon a time there was place called Sam-sam-sa-mara. The animals and the people lived and worked together like they didn't know they weren't supposed to.

There was a little boy in Sam-sam-sa-mara whose name was Sam. Sam's mama was also named Sam. So was Sam's daddy. In fact, all the little boys and little girls and mamas and daddies were named Sam. But nobody ever got confused about which Sam was which, and that's why nobody was named Joleen or Natisha or Willie.

SAM AND THE TIGERS: FIFTH DRAFT (10/31/95)

Once upon a time there was place called Sam-sam-sa-mara.

There was a little boy in Sam-sam-sa-mara whose name was Sam. Sam's mama was also named Sam. So was Sam's daddy. In fact, all the little boys and little girls and mamas and daddies were named Sam. But nobody ever got confused about which Sam was which, and that's why nobody was named Joleen or Natisha or Willie.

SAM AND THE TIGERS: SIXTH DRAFT (11/16/95) - LESTER

Once upon a time in a place called Sam-sam-sa-mara the animals and the people lived together like they didn't know they weren't supposed to.

There was a little boy in Sam-sam-sa-mara named Sam. Sam's mama was also named Sam. So was Sam's daddy. In fact, all the little boys and little girls and mamas and daddies were named Sam. But nobody ever got confused about which Sam was which, and that's why nobody was named Joleen or Natisha or Willie.

The opening lines of four of Lester's six draft manuscripts.
The first draft, upper left, is dated May 1995.

to revise his manuscript, "mostly cutting, hammering down." Lester produced six drafts of *Sam and the Tigers* before at last feeling satisfied.

Dial published *Sam and the Tigers* in September of 1996. By a strange coincidence, a second retelling of the Bannerman book, Fred Marcellino's *The Story of Little Babaji,* was published by HarperCollins that same month. Pinkney and Lester had not known beforehand about Marcellino's book and Marcellino had not known about theirs. Noting the odd turn of events, many newspapers and magazines reviewed the two versions together, giving the books even more attention than either one might have received on its own. Reviewers were divided as to which version they liked better, but, surprisingly, only a few critics questioned the decision to retell and reillustrate *The Story of Little Black Sambo.* Some even took the simultaneous appearance of the two versions as a sign that the time must somehow have been right for a new retelling. Brief statements by Lester and Pinkney, explaining

Finished art by Pinkney for the scene in which the tigers argue
about which one of them looks "the finest."

why they had wanted to redo Bannerman's story, may also have helped. To everyone's great relief, the uproar that Pinkney, Lester, and Fogelman had expected did
not occur.

Sam and the Tigers proved to be a special book for the artist and writer. While
photographing his grandson, Pinkney had been touched to see "how well Myles
related to the story—much as I had as a boy." Lester took satisfaction in the thought
of having "given back" the story to readers who had grown up with mixed feelings
about it. Lester was also glad to have had the chance to "present the story to the two
generations [younger than himself] who, because the book had been widely banned
from the sixties onward, had grown up not knowing it at all." This group of new
readers included his own son. He dedicated the text "To the Internet," the still-new,
computer-age tool that had drawn him into a rethinking of The Story of Little Black
Sambo in the first place.

Working on Sam and the Tigers also strengthened Pinkney and Lester's bond as collaborators. "Julius's storytelling voice," Pinkney says, "allowed me to create pictures that did not just mimic the text but were inspired by it."

"We discovered all over again," says Lester, "that there was no ego competition between us. And we realized that what we both most cared about was the book."

Some Books Written by Julius Lester and Illustrated by Jerry Pinkney

1987	*The Tales of Uncle Remus: The Adventures of Brer Rabbit* (Dial)
1988	*More Tales of Uncle Remus: Further Adventures of Brer Rabbit, His Friends, Enemies, and Others* (Dial)
1989	*Further Tales of Uncle Remus: The Misadventures of Brer Rabbit, Brer Fox, Brer Wolf, the Doodang, and Other Creatures* (Dial)
1994	*The Last Tales of Uncle Remus* (Dial)
1994	*John Henry* (Dial)
1996	*Sam and the Tigers: A New Telling of Little Black Sambo* (Dial)
1997	*Black Cowboy, Wild Horses: A True Story* (Dial)
1999	*Uncle Remus: The Complete Tales* (Phyllis Fogelman Books)
2000	*Albidaro and the Mischievous Dream* (Phyllis Fogelman Books)

Joanna Cole

(born August 11, 1944, Newark, New Jersey)

and

Bruce Degen

(born June 14, 1945, Brooklyn, New York)

*THE MAGIC
SCHOOL BUS
EXPLORES THE SENSES*
(Scholastic, 1999)

*Art medium: watercolor
and pen and ink*

Bruce Degen and
Joanna Cole

In 1985, Joanna Cole had been a children's-book writer for fifteen years and had published scores of notable science books for kids, as well as many humorous picture books. That same year, Craig Walker, an editor at Scholastic, had a very good idea for a book. Walker wanted to publish a picture book about a class trip, with a story that worked as a science lesson but would also make readers laugh. He wondered whether Cole might want to write such a book.

Until then, most children's science books had been written in a no-nonsense style, with illustrations to match. Knowing this, Cole hesitated. She worried that librarians and teachers might be put off by a lighter approach to dinosaurs and digestion.

But Cole was also intrigued. "I was excited by the challenge Craig had offered me: doing a funny storybook that would also be a serious science book," says Cole. "So I wrote the book and made a rough dummy and it was a terribly complicated

Double-page spread from Degen's dummy for *The Magic School Bus at the Waterworks.*

thing—all words with hardly any room left for the illustrations. We *really* needed a great illustrator to make visual sense out of it."

Cole had deliberately chosen a subject—the story of how our drinking water reaches us—that schoolchildren might think was going to be dull. Part of the fun of *The Magic School Bus at the Waterworks* (1986) would lie in the discovery that this was not so. She gave the class teacher a silly-sounding name and an old-fashioned manner that concealed another surprise for readers: Ms. Frizzle was one daredevilishly wild and adventurous grown-up!

Since a real teacher could not take a class to the places Ms. Frizzle would take hers, Cole added the element of magic. In the *Waterworks* book, the bus begins to rise into the air as it zooms over a bridge, and—*voilà!*—the bus, the teacher, and the entire class evaporate. Later, the bus magically reappears in the school parking lot, as good as new.

While researching the water cycle, Cole had uncovered a great many fascinating facts and was unwilling, at first, to leave out any of them. As her text grew longer, however, she realized she needed to save space somehow. That was when she first thought to put her characters' conversations in cartoon-style word balloons. Recalling her own enjoyment of grade-school science-report writing, Cole decided it might also be fun—and shorten the text still more—to include "pages" from her characters' fact-filled class reports in each illustration.

Cole, who had once been a children's-book editor herself, realized that her plan to blend the text and pictures closely together meant that she and the illustrator—whoever it was—would have to work as a team. It was at about this time that Craig Walker telephoned Bruce Degen.

"How would you like to illustrate a book for which you will have to do an enormous amount of research," Walker began, "and work harder than you have ever worked before—and it will be *horrible?*"

Degen, a former schoolteacher with more than twenty-five books to his credit, replied, "Why would I want to do that?"

"Because we'll pay you a lot of money."

"When do I start?" asked the artist. In those days, both Degen and Cole were struggling to make a living as freelancers, and as Cole likes to say, "The wolf was often at the door."

A few days later, Degen, Cole, and Walker had their first meeting.

Walker chose Degen because, as the illustrator of Jane Yolen's Commander Toad series of fantasies, he had shown the ability to draw spaceships, animals, and other science-related subjects with a lively sense of fun. At the meeting, Degen made sketches to suggest how Cole's text might be made to fit on the page. He showed that long horizontal pages worked better than the tall vertical ones of Cole's dummy. Because the fact-filled pages were bound to look a bit cluttered, he stressed that the important thing was to make it clear to readers exactly what each drawing and set of words had to do with those around it. "We knew it wasn't going to be a pretty picture!" Degen recalls with a laugh.

Degen and Cole, who were meeting that day for the first time, found that they liked each other. Degen's warm, outgoing manner and Cole's sly sense of fun were a good match. They admired each other's skill and professionalism.

This did not mean, however, that they would decide to meet *often*. Degen knew he did not want a writer looking over his shoulder. Cole, who describes herself as

In this detail from Degen's *Senses* dummy, a playful pretend ad features a portrait of Cole.

"very detail-oriented," knew she wanted to resist the temptation to do so. It felt better to both of them to let Walker and assistant editor Phoebe Yeh be in the middle and pass ideas and questions between the author and illustrator. In all, Cole and Degen had two long work sessions before *The Magic School Bus at the Waterworks* was done, and they kept to this pattern for each of the nine sequels that followed. But with their editors as go-betweens, they traded ideas all the time.

Cole chose the subject of each Magic School Bus book and completed her manuscript before sending it to Degen. She often took a year to do so. Then, following their first face-to-face discussion, Cole sent Degen a boxful of reference materials, with pages marked to indicate diagrams or photographs that might be of special help to him.

Next, drawing in pencil, Degen would make a detailed dummy. During this stage, it often became clear when Cole had tried to fit too much information onto a page, or when more information was needed to make a point clearly. "Layers and layers of revision followed," Degen says, as sketches and rewrites passed back and forth.

In the very beginning, of course, no one knew just what Ms. Frizzle would look like. Degen made a series of sketches to test out different possibilities. Cole and the editors studied the sketches and gave their opinions.

Cole had pictured someone like her own junior-high-school science teacher. "Miss Bair did not do crazy things. She dressed conservatively. She did not take her class on field trips. But like Ms. Frizzle and her class, Miss Bair always plunged

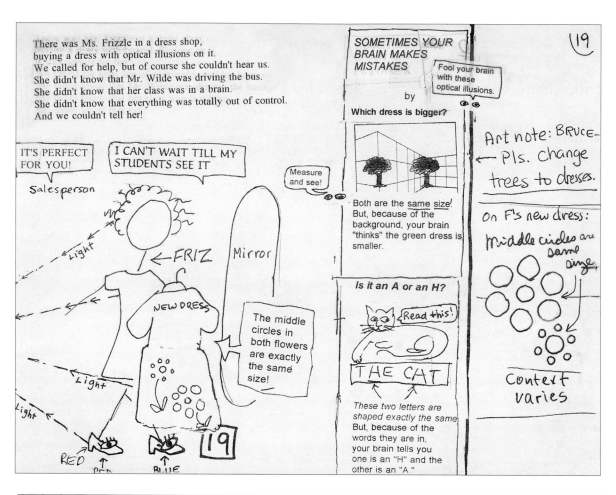

Page from Cole's dummy for *The Magic School Bus Explores the Senses*, with notes in the right-hand margin for Degen and rare examples of the author's own drawing.

Degen's detailed dummy rendering of the same page.

ahead in her enthusiasm for her subject, while we kids hurried to catch up. I loved that about her."

Degen's model was his tenth-grade geometry teacher, a short, curly-haired woman named Miss Isaacs, who positively glowed with love for the beauty of math and who, Degen recalls, "inspired her definitely nonmathematical student—me."

Gradually, the collaborators' various ideas about their central character began to merge. In her *Waterworks* dummy, Cole had written that Ms. Frizzle wore "strange dresses and shoes." Degen decided to keep Ms. Frizzle in a plain dress of the same old-fashioned design, and to change only the fabric pattern from illustration to illustration. Each new pattern became an enjoyable surprise, as did the wildly amusing earrings and shoes that Degen designed for her.

Cole gave Degen a good deal of freedom. She provided text for every word balloon but, except for Ms. Frizzle and Arnold, did not specify which class member was to speak which lines. As Degen continued to draw the characters, he began to "know" which of them was likeliest to say any given line. "I decided, for example, that if there was a sarcastic comment, it would most often be Amanda Jane—the blonde with the little pageboy—who said it."

When Degen had space left over in an illustration, he sometimes filled it with a few words of his own. As the bus starts to shrink in *The Magic School Bus Explores the Senses*, a bit of Degen doggerel—"Shakey-Quakey/Shrinky/Dinky/Itsy/Bitsy/Teeny/Weeny"—appears in the bus's destination window.

"I sometimes make him take out things like that," Cole says. "Bruce can have the final say about the pictures, but as the writer I have veto power over the words in the book. But if I like what he writes, then it stays."

The Magic School Bus Explores the Senses was the tenth book in what, early on, became an enormously popular series. By the time the third book, *The Magic School Bus Inside the Human Body* (1989), was published, Cole and Degen were attracting around-the-block lines of fans at bookstores throughout the United States. "It was absolutely wild," Degen says. "We felt almost like the Beatles."

In 1994, the same year that the sixth book, *The Magic School Bus in the Time of the Dinosaurs*, was published, a Public Broadcasting System show based on the series made its debut, with Cole and Degen serving as advisers. (The series later moved to the Fox Kids Network.) Their books were also being translated into more and more

Degen and Cole on tour following the publication
of *The Magic School Bus in the Time of the Dinosaurs,* 1994.

languages (including Spanish, German, Italian, Hebrew, Arabic, Greek, Portuguese, Japanese, and Korean) and published in more and more countries throughout the world. By the time *The Magic School Bus Explores the Senses* appeared in March 1999, more than 16 million copies of the books had been sold.

"It all felt so strange," Cole recalls. "I had written so many other books by then, and of course none of the others had received anything like that kind of attention. Science-book writers didn't get lines around the corner. Science-book writers often didn't even get their books in stores! It took time to adjust to what was happening. And that is when Bruce and I really became friends, as we traveled to more and more bookstores and schools and libraries and conventions."

Although the Magic School Bus books are alike in many ways, each of Cole's manuscripts presented Degen with new visual problems to solve. In the *Senses* book, for example, the eye that the school bus "explores" belongs to a motorcycle police-man. Cole's text called for the bus to go sailing out the eye and into the ear of a passing child. The problem for Degen was that motorcycle policemen always wear sunglasses. How could the bus possibly clear the glasses on its way to the ear? "I said, 'Change it to a regular policeman, who might not be wearing glasses,'" Degen recalls. "But Joanna said: 'No! That's impossible!'"

"Of course, he *had* to be a motorcycle policeman," Cole explains, "to be trailing Ms. Frizzle's car in that scene. So I asked Bruce, 'Why does he *have* to wear glasses?'" "Because motorcycle policemen *always* do," had been Degen's response. Eventually, Degen slid the glasses partway down the bridge of the officer's nose so that a very small bus—a magic one, anyway—could make it over the frame.

Problems like this one were minor, however, compared with the challenge of creating scientifically accurate drawings of, say, the interior of a human brain with a school bus cruising around inside it.

"We had a lot of trouble with the brain," Cole recalls with a grin. The brain's pivotal role in sensory experience was the main concept around which all the myriad facts in the book were organized. "We kept coming back to the brain," Cole says, "in

Degen's dummy drawing showing the bus exiting Officer Jones's eye.

A typically complex page design, featuring drawings of characters in action,
a cutaway view, class reports, and a "Frizzle Fact."

order to show that it's really there that we see, taste, touch, smell, and hear."

"Because the brain is so complex," says Degen, "it was necessary to simplify the art while keeping it accurate, to decide what visual details would help kids understand the concept." A professional scientist helped at this and other stages to ensure that text and illustrations were factually correct as well as clear.

As the Magic School Bus series grew, both Cole and Degen came to feel they knew their characters better. Ms. Frizzle did not have a first name (Valerie) until the sixth book, *The Magic School Bus in the Time of the Dinosaurs*. In *The Magic School Bus Explores the Senses*, the school's assistant principal, Mr. Wilde, appears for the first time, as do Ms. Frizzle's mother and her car. Each of these new story elements required additional thought and drawing.

Cole and Degen agree that a lovely bonus that came out of writing and illustrating the books is to have been put in touch with so many dedicated teachers. "In every school we have visited," says Cole, "there has always been one teacher who told us, 'I'm the *real* Ms. Frizzle of this school'—the teacher who wants to get the kids involved in what they're learning." Teachers once afraid to teach science said that, with the help of these books, they now enjoyed doing so. Others told them that children with learning disabilities and those just learning English readily grasped the Magic School Bus books, with their closely linked text and pictures. Older children with reading difficulties responded to the clever, unbabyish humor.

Sketch by Degen for Ms. Frizzle's car.

Having completed ten series volumes in all and contributed to countless spin-offs, from television shows to children's backpacks and Ms. Frizzle dolls, both collaborators felt ready for another challenge. For years, teachers and parents had been asking for books on social studies topics. To explore that field, Cole and Degen now began a new series about Ms. Frizzle on vacation, narrated by the unpredictable teacher herself. The new books, starting with *Ms. Frizzle's Adventures: Ancient Egypt* (2001), would double as time-travel tales. For a teacher who had already squeezed inside a raindrop, toured a human lung, and roamed the entire solar system, the new adventures seemed to make perfect sense. As Cole says, "When the Friz takes a vacation, it's not going to be any ordinary day at the beach."

Collaboration rarely ever is either.

Some Books Written by Joanna Cole and Illustrated by Bruce Degen

1986   *The Magic School Bus at the Waterworks* (Scholastic)

1987   *The Magic School Bus Inside the Earth* (Scholastic)

1989   *The Magic School Bus Inside the Human Body* (Scholastic)

1990   *The Magic School Bus Lost in the Solar System* (Scholastic)

1992   *The Magic School Bus on the Ocean Floor* (Scholastic)

1994   *The Magic School Bus in the Time of the Dinosaurs* (Scholastic)

1995   *The Magic School Bus Inside a Hurricane* (Scholastic)

1996   *The Magic School Bus Inside a Beehive* (Scholastic)

1997   *The Magic School Bus and the Electric Field Trip* (Scholastic)

1999   *The Magic School Bus Explores the Senses* (Scholastic)

2001   *Ms. Frizzle's Adventures: Ancient Egypt* (Scholastic)

Glossary

animator An artist who, starting with a series of drawings or other still images, makes films or videos in which things appear to move.

art director One of the people at a publishing house who hires and oversees the work of designers.

Braque, Georges (1882–1963) The French painter who teamed up with Pablo Picasso during the early years of the twentieth century, in Paris, to invent a new kind of painting called Cubism.

caricature A portrait or other likeness that exaggerates certain of its subject's features (the nose or chin, for example), usually for the sake of making fun of that person.

collaboration Work done by partners or teammates toward a common goal.

coming-of-age story A story in which a young hero becomes more grown up as a result of his or her experiences.

copyright page A page placed just after the title page of a book, on which is stated the year of publication of the book, the legal owner or "copyright holder" of its text and illustrations, and other details of its creation and history.

critic [also, **reviewer**] A writer, often for a newspaper or magazine, whose job is to say what he or she thinks of newly published books.

deadline The day when a completed book or other piece of work is due at the publishing house.

designer One of the people at a publishing house who is responsible for deciding about such visual matters as the choice of type and the overall look of each printed page.

dummy A handmade book created by an illustrator as a model and plan for a picture book on which he or she is beginning work.

editor One of the people at a publishing company who is responsible for choosing which books the house will publish and for helping the writers and illustrators involved to revise and finish their work.

Gogol, Nikolai (1809–52) A Russian writer of stories and novels that combine elements of fantasy and everyday life.

gouache A type of water-based paint that leaves solid or "opaque" marks on the page.

hand-lettering Text written out by hand when a more personal feeling is wanted than could be gotten by setting the same piece of text in type.

hieroglyphics An ancient system of writing using picture symbols instead of alphabet letters.

influence Anyone or anything from which a writer or artist learns a lesson that helps to shape his or her work.

inspiration Anyone or anything that gives a writer or artist the urge to create, or a clearer idea of what it is that he or she wishes to create.

Kafka, Franz (1883–1924) A Jewish writer, born in Prague, whose powerful fables have the eerie clarity of nightmares.

layout The arrangement of illustrations and type on a printed page.

manuscript A piece of writing to be submitted for publication.

medieval illuminated manuscript One of the books lovingly lettered and illustrated by hand, by European monks, during the centuries before the invention, in 1455, of the modern printing press.

parody [also, **spoof**] A humorous version of a story or poem meant to poke fun at the original.

Picasso, Pablo (1881–1973) A Spanish-born painter who, while living in Paris during the early years of the twentieth century, collaborated with Georges Braque to invent a new style of art called Cubism.

portfolio A small selection of an illustrator's best work for showing to publishers and others who might wish to hire the artist.

Rembrandt van Rijn (1606–69) A Dutch artist famous for his ability to capture the effects of light and shadow in his paintings and prints.

research A deeper look into any subject. Reading, close observation, and talking with knowledgeable persons are some ways to do research.

revision A reworking of a piece of writing or art to make it better.

sketch A rough drawing made by an artist as a step toward creating a finished piece of art.

stereotype An oversimplified image or idea that distorts, or completely misses, the truth about its subject.

studio A room or other well-lighted space for art-making.

surrealistic Strange in a dreamlike way.

table of contents A page placed near the beginning of a book, listing its chapters (or stories or poems), in order of appearance, and their page numbers.

thumbnail sketch The first, very rough drawing or drawings that illustrators often make when starting work on a book.

title page One of the first pages of a book, on which the title of the book is stated along with the names of its author, illustrator, and publisher.

type Alphabet letters, numbers, and other characters specially designed for use in the printing of books, newspapers, magazines, posters, and the like.

word balloon In comic books and strips, an oval or other outline containing the words that a character is thinking or saying.

working title A temporary title, used by the author and others to refer to a work-in-progress until a title that feels just right is found.

Index